5-14

D0125519

JUNIOR
BIOGRAPHY
FROM
ANCIENT
CIVILIZATIONS

ARCHIMEDES

CLAIRE O'NEAL

Mitchell Lane
PUBLISHERS

P.O. Box 196
Hockessin, Delaware 19707
Visit us on the web: www.mitchelllane.com
Comments? Email us: mitchelllane@mitchelllane.com

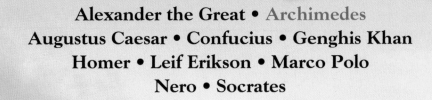

JUNIOR BIOGRAPHY FROM
ANCIENT CIVILIZATIONS

Alexander the Great • Archimedes
Augustus Caesar • Confucius • Genghis Khan
Homer • Leif Erikson • Marco Polo
Nero • Socrates

Copyright © 2014 by Mitchell Lane Publishers

Printing   1   2   3   4   5   6   7   8   9

ABOUT THE AUTHOR: Claire O'Neal has published over two dozen books with Mitchell Lane in addition to professional scientific papers. She holds degrees in English and biology from Indiana University, and a Ph.D. in chemistry from the University of Washington. Claire first learned about Archimedes in her high school geometry class. She now enjoys recreating Archimedes' experiments, especially in costume, with her husband and two young sons in Delaware.

PUBLISHER'S NOTE: The facts on which the story in this book is based have been thoroughly researched. Documentation of such research can be found on pages 44–46. While every possible effort has been made to ensure accuracy, the publisher will not assume liability for damages caused by inaccuracies in the data, and makes no warranty on the accuracy of the information contained herein.

Library of Congress
Cataloging-in-Publication Data

O'Neal, Claire.
  Archimedes / by Claire O'Neal.
    pages cm. — (Junior biography from ancient civilizations)
  Audience: 8–11.
  Audience: Grade 4 to 6.
  Includes bibliographical references and index.
  ISBN 978-1-61228-437-8 (library bound)
  1. Archimedes—Biography—Juvenile literature. 2. Mathematicians—Greece--Biography—Juvenile literature. 3. Mathematics, Ancient—Juvenile literature. 4. Mathematics—Study and teaching (Elementary) I. Title.
  QA29.A7O54 2014
  510.92—dc23
  [B]
                              2013012549

eBook ISBN: 9781612284996

                                        PLB

CONTENTS

Phonetic pronunciations of words in **bold**
can be found on page 46.

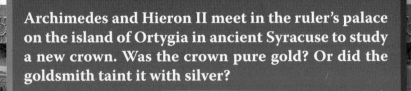

Archimedes and Hieron II meet in the ruler's palace on the island of Ortygia in ancient Syracuse to study a new crown. Was the crown pure gold? Or did the goldsmith taint it with silver?

CHAPTER 1
Eureka!

Hieron* II should have been proud, delighted even, with his new golden crown. He had carefully measured out the gold from his personal treasure and handed it to a master goldsmith. The man returned with a true work of art—a shining yellow crown shaped like a laurel wreath, a symbol of victory. Hieron intended to place it in his temples as a present to the gods who had given him glory as the ruler of **Syracuse**.

But Hieron was suspicious. He heard a rumor that the goldsmith had stolen some of the gold. The crown was exactly the weight it should be, but what if the goldsmith had mixed a little silver into the crown and pocketed some of Hieron's gold for himself? Hieron sent for a wise and trusted friend. "Archimedes," Hieron asked, "Can you test this wreath to see if it is pure gold without damaging it?"

It was just the kind of riddle **Archimedes** loved—and the kind that turned his servants into horrible nags. Their absent-minded master often got so lost in his own thoughts that they had to remind him to take care of himself. They tried to

*For pronunciations of words in **bold**, see page 46.

put Archimedes to bed, only to find him still awake in the morning, tracing equations in the spent fire's ashes.

Hieron's request frustrated Archimedes. He couldn't figure out a way of determining if Hieron's suspicions were correct. He refused to dress and eat, and insisted he had no time for taking a bath. Finally his servants grew tired of his stinking and dragged him to Syracuse's bath house. Annoyed at the interruption, Archimedes refused to stop working, even as the servants slathered him with bathing oils. He continued scratching shapes in the suds on his skin. Reluctantly, Archimedes sank into the warm, deep tub. Perhaps distracted from arguing with their master, his servants had filled it too full. Hot water sloshed over the sides, splashing onto the tile floor. The sound jarred Archimedes out of his mathematical daydream. He stood up; the water level went down. He lowered his body carefully into the water and watched the water level rise once more.

"**Eureka**!" he screamed. The great thinker had the answer to Hieron's question. Archimedes leaped from the tub, pushing past his startled servants, and ran straight to Hieron's palace. He couldn't be bothered with clothes or shoes. The citizens of Syracuse had to laugh at their resident genius streaking through the town naked, shouting with joy at his discovery: "Eureka! I have found it!"

Archimedes' discovery—as well as the answer to Hieron's riddle— had to do with specific gravity, or the weight of any object in relation to the weight of the same amount, or volume, of water. When an object is in a liquid like water, the liquid moves to surround the object. The level of the liquid moves up, or becomes displaced, by the extra space the object takes up.

How would the crown measure up in its own "Eureka" bath? Archimedes dunked the golden wreath in a tub full of water, measuring the amount of water that spilled over. Next, Archimedes repeated the dunking test, but this time with a pure gold brick borrowed from Hieron's treasury. The crown and the brick weighed

Archimedes repeated his bath with different materials in different shapes to sort out his laws of buoyancy. You can repeat his experiment yourself—measure some water in a glass measuring cup and add different objects, one at a time, to see what happens to the level of the liquid.

exactly the same. Archimedes knew that liquids do not care about the shape of an object, flowing around all submerged shapes. If the crown really was pure gold, like the brick, the two objects would displace the same amount of water. But the brick displaced *less* water than the crown. That's because the many curves of the laurel leaves were slightly larger than they would have been if they had been only made of pure gold. When Archimedes shared his findings with Hieron, the angry ruler ordered his soldiers to *displace* the goldsmith's head.

Inspired by his discovery, Archimedes experimented tirelessly until he had worked out the laws of buoyancy. Any seagoing Syracuse citizen knew that certain things—such as wood—floated no matter how much they weighed. On the other hand, they knew that stones and chunks of iron always sank. Archimedes concluded that "Any floating object displaces its own *weight* of fluid."[1] For any object that sinks, such as Hieron's golden wreath, the *volume* of the object displaces an equal *volume* of water. Archimedes' pen flew as he told his mathematical friends of his discovery in a treatise he called *On Floating Bodies*. It long had been obvious that ships floated. Now—for the first time in history—Archimedes understood why. These two rules, known as Archimedes' Principle, are still used today.

A mathematician, engineer, and inventor, Archimedes was one of the most creative and brilliant minds in the ancient world, and perhaps in all of human history. He discovered how to use math to explain the world around him in ways no one ever had before. His findings revolutionized math, physics, and engineering for all time, buoying every scientist since.

Archimedes, sculpted by Simon-Louis Boquet in 1788, sits in the Louvre Museum in Paris

The Greatest of the Greek Cities

The population of ancient Greece began to explode in the 7th and 8th centuries BCE. The people soon suffered from famine and overcrowding. Some of the braver Greeks took to their ships to find a better life elsewhere around the Mediterranean. Many looked to the coasts of southern Italy, bringing their language and culture with them.

In 733 or 734 BCE, citizens from the Greek city of **Corinth** sailed to a harbor on the eastern shore of the island of **Sicily**. They made their first home on a tiny island, named **Ortygia**, separated from Sicily's coast by a thin channel. Their leader, **Archias**, named the new settlement Sirako, which is Greek for "salt marsh." With fertile land and friendly native tribes, the city quickly outgrew Ortygia.

Syracusans founded more colonies throughout the island of Sicily, and soon the entire island embraced Greek language and culture. Thanks to Syracuse's strategic position as a port in the middle of the Mediterranean Sea, the city became one of the major powers of the Mediterranean world, or, according to **Cicero**, "the greatest of the Greek cities, and the most beautiful of them all."[2]

Kings of Syracuse were given the title of Tyrant. Hieron II, the Tyrant when Archimedes lived, ruled from 270 to 215 BCE. Today we call rulers who rule unfairly or violently "tyrants." But in ancient Greece, "Tyrant" simply meant "ruler of a city-state," and was often used to describe someone who came to power using military muscle.

Important Ancient Cities

A collector's card of Archimedes—from a Belgian chocolate company in 1965—shows the mathematician with an analytic balance. This type of scale, still in use today, uses Archimedes' law of the lever to compare the weights of two groups of objects.

CHAPTER 2
The Birth of a Thinker

Passers-by on the narrow streets of Syracuse might have smiled to notice an olive branch hanging on Phidias's door. It was a sign of his new son's name day. Phidias proudly introduced the infant to friends and family. He was called Archimedes, which meant "master of thought."

Phidias, an astronomer, raised his son in a home of science. Phidias would have passed down the era's mathematical knowledge, from Egypt and Babylon, to the young Archimedes. Phidias might have also showed him how to use math to chart the movements of the five planets the Greeks could see with the naked eye—Mercury, Venus, Mars, Jupiter, and Saturn—and to study the size and paths of the sun and moon.

Archimedes probably began school when he was eight, like other boys of Syracuse. Students walked to the house of a paid teacher. They learned reading and writing, and also religion and history, by memorizing and reciting the long poems of Homer. They scratched their math lessons on wax-covered boards, or traced letters and numbers in dirt or sand. When most boys were about 14, they became apprentices to men like shipbuilders or doctors, to learn how to make money on their own. Boys from wealthy families had no such need. They began a life in government, going to the town center with their fathers and listening to older men talk politics.

Archimedes followed a new and different path. The promising young scholar left Syracuse to study in Alexandria, the capital of Egypt. Egyptian king Ptolemy I invited brilliant minds to Alexandria, mathematicians and astronomers, as well as the greatest writers, speakers, and philosophers. He provided palace-like buildings and beautiful gardens for them, and paid them just to work on their favorite mental challenges.

The jewel of **Ptolemy**'s university was the Library, the largest and most spectacular of its kind for centuries to come. To be the head librarian, literally in charge of all the knowledge in the world, was a high honor indeed. **Eratosthenes** of **Cyrene** (276–194 BCE) was head librarian in Archimedes' time. Later known as the Father of Geography, Eratosthenes knew that the Earth was round and calculated its circumference. He also invented a system of latitude and longitude when he drafted a map of the Earth. Eratosthenes and Archimedes became lifelong friends.

Archimedes and Eratosthenes studied the latest discoveries of Greek math experts like **Euclid** of Alexandria (ca. 325–265 BCE). Euclid created a precise new mathematical language to state obvious truths, or postulates.[1] In his masterwork, *The Elements*, Euclid showed how to use postulates to prove whether more complicated ideas were math fact or math fiction. Euclid also organized shapes into two groups: flat shapes (circles, squares, triangles) and solid shapes (spheres, cones, cylinders, cubes). The elegance of Euclid's math appealed to Archimedes, whose greatest joy was to study shapes.

At night, Archimedes and Eratosthenes explored the stars from the Library's observatory. Archimedes would later design and build a model planetarium. He fashioned the planets, the sun, and the moon,

Eratosthenes measured the Earth's circumference using simple geometry.

Eratosthenes knew that the sun shone directly overhead on the first day of summer in Syene, a city in southeast Egypt. At Alexandria (A) at the same time, the sun's position was not directly overhead, but off by a small angle (φ). Eratosthenes measured φ to be $\frac{1}{50}$ of a circle. Then he multiplied these fifty parts of a circle times the distance (δ) between the cities—5,000 stadia—to find that the circumference of the Earth must be 250,000 stadia. Disagreement among historians about the length of a stadion in today's units means that Eratosthenes' answer lies somewhere between 24,388 miles (39,250 kilometers) to 32,467 miles (52,250 kilometers). Whichever estimate you use, Eratosthenes' answer is remarkably close to the actual value of 24,901 miles (40,075 kilometers).

and engineered them to move in their regular orbits, powered by water. Archimedes' planetarium predicted their positions so accurately that it could forecast eclipses of the sun and moon.[2]

For fun, Archimedes and his friends probably took sailing trips on the majestic Nile River. They would have seen the difficult work of farming along the river. To keep their crops from withering in the hot sun, farmers and their families carried buckets of water from the Nile to irrigation ditches, emptied them, then returned to the river in an exhausting, constant march that lasted for much of the day.

Archimedes wondered if he could ease the farmers' burden. He built a large wooden screw, then encased it tightly inside a hollow wooden cylinder. Archimedes tilted the cylinder at the Nile's edge.

An Archimedes screw transports water uphill with the simple turn of a crank. These machines today continue to move things that water pumps cannot—like fish, thick liquids at sewage treatment plants, or small and loose materials like grains or beads in a factory.

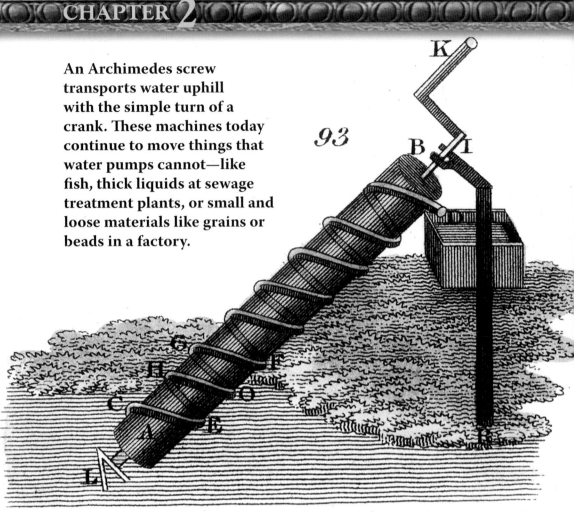

One end lay in the water, the other end lay over land. Using a crank, farmers would turn the screw inside the cylinder case. The turning screw threads carried water up from the river like a liquid elevator and dumped it out the dry end of the machine. Now the water could flow quickly and easily into the fields.[3] Some farmers along the Nile still use Archimedes' Screw today, and it remains an essential tool on farms where electricity may not be available. Back in Syracuse, Hieron's shipbuilders installed Archimedes' Screws inside their boats to purge water from leaky hulls.

Perhaps sailing made Archimedes' heart long for home. At some point he returned to Syracuse. He would never leave his native city again.

The Library of Alexandria

Ptolemy I built the Mouseion—or Museum—of Alexandria as a research institute. His son, Ptolemy II, added the Library. Like other libraries at the time, scholars were welcome to visit and read from its stacks of scrolls, or to make their own copies to take home for personal study.

The Library of Alexandria became the best-known and complete collection of written works in the ancient world. Ptolemy II saw to that. His government passed a law: all foreign ships docked in Alexandria could not leave until Library scribes had made copies of any scrolls they carried.

The Library of Alexandria survived through fire, war, and natural disaster until the 7th century CE. Rome's Julius Caesar accidentally burned part of the Library when he came conquering in 48 BCE. The Library's scribes restored it. Alexandria was hit hard by a massive tsunami in 365, then by violent Christians who attacked the Library during a riot several decades later. Again, the Library's scribes restored the collection.

But they could not withstand Islamic armies from Baghdad (in modern-day Iraq) who took the city in 642 CE. The new ruler, Caliph Omar, ordered his troops to burn all the scrolls from the Library to heat water for the city's public baths.[4]

Archimedes, painted in 1630 by Italian artist Jusepe de Ribera (1591–1652).

CHAPTER 3
Give Me a Place to Stand...

Many of Archimedes' mathematical works today seem simple and obvious, but in his day his work was groundbreaking. For example, people had known for thousands of years how to estimate the circumference of a circle. Simply multiply the distance across the circle at its widest point—the diameter—by about three. Archimedes was determined to find a more accurate answer.

He drew two hexagons—six-sided figures—around a circle. One fit just inside the circle, each of its corners contacting the circle's line. The other skimmed the outside of the circle, with the center of each edge touching the circle. Archimedes could measure the perimeter of each hexagon, and he knew the value of the circle's circumference lay between these two numbers. But Archimedes also knew that a shape with a greater number of sides would better fit the shape of the circle. He doubled the number of sides of each hexagon again and again, stopping when the shapes had 96 sides. Now he knew that history's estimate of "about three" should really be between $3^{10}/_{71}$ (3.1408) and $3^{1}/_{7}$ (3.1429). Archimedes went on

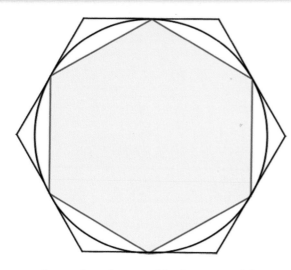

Archimedes used two hexagons as boundaries for the circumference of a circle. The smaller hexagon is inscribed within the circle (meaning its corners touch the circle). The larger hexagon circumscribes the circle (meaning the hexagon's flat edges touch the circle).

to show that he could also use this same special number to find the area of a circle.

In 1706, British mathematician William Jones gave Archimedes' special number a name. He called it pi, using the Greek letter "*p*" [π] as in "*perimeter*."[1] Archimedes' calculations are amazingly close to the actual value of *pi*, even to the ten-thousandth decimal place (3.14159).

Archimedes loved to think about curved shapes. He bent lines around in his head to create spirals, such as in snail shells. He sliced up cones at different angles to create curves he named *ellipse, parabola,* and *hyperbola.*[2] He rolled rectangles and squares into cylinders and spun circles into spheres. He also discovered how to calculate the area and volume of these objects. Archimedes begged his friends to engrave his proudest discovery on his tombstone—that the volume of a sphere is exactly ⅔ the volume of a cylinder that fits perfectly around it.

Amazingly, Archimedes developed his ideas in spite of the complicated Greek number system. The largest number in the Greek system was *M*, a *myriad*, which today we know as ten thousand. Archimedes wondered just how high numbers could go. The Greeks knew of numbers as large as a *myriad myriads*—or one hundred million. Archimedes wondered just how high could numbers go.

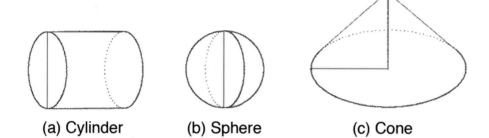

(a) Cylinder   (b) Sphere   (c) Cone

Archimedes discovered how to find the surface area and volume of cylinders, spheres, and cones, among other shapes. We still use his equations today.

(A) Cylinder volume = area of the base circle x height = [pi]r²h
(B) Sphere volume = ⁴⁄₃ x radius x area of a center circle = [pi]r³
(C) Cone volume = ⅓ x area of the base circle x height = ⅓ [pi]r²h

He invented a mathematical language of multiplying *myriads* to count very large numbers. One *myriad* (*M*), then a *myriad myriads* (*M* times *M*), then a *myriad myriad myriads* (*M* times *M* times *M*, or one trillion)—and still he continued. The largest number he "counted" to is even larger than a googol, written as a 1 with 100 zeroes behind it. Archimedes used this system to calculate that, given the size of the Earth, the Moon, and the Sun, the universe could hold about 8×10^{63} grains of sand (that's written as an 8 with 63 zeroes behind it.).[3] Over 2,000 years later, British astrophysicist Arthur Eddington calculated that the universe contained about 10^{80} atoms. Scientists were shocked at Archimedes' close guess.

Meanwhile, Archimedes' royal friend had bigger problems than counting grains of sand. Hieron commissioned a magnificent new ship, the *Syracusia*, for Ptolemy II. But the enormous vessel sat on land, useless. All of Hieron's palace slaves working together could not drag the 2,000-ton *Syracusia* into the harbor.[4] The king announced a public challenge to his genius friend: Could Archimedes use math to do what men could not?

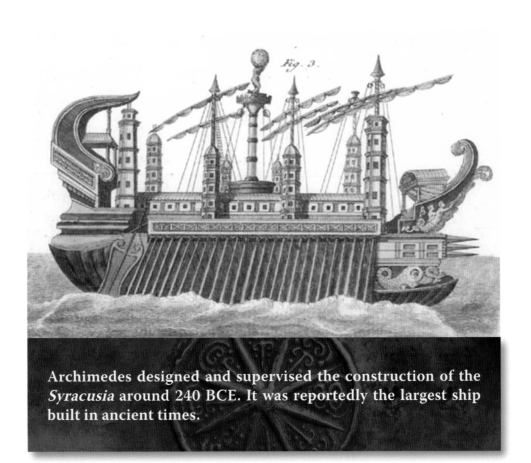

Archimedes designed and supervised the construction of the *Syracusia* around 240 BCE. It was reportedly the largest ship built in ancient times.

Any worker lifting heavy cargo knew how to use levers and ramps. But Archimedes was the first to discover *why* these simple machines work. For a lever to balance, objects on both sides have two properties that must equal each other when multiplied together: their weight, and their distance from the lever's pivot point, or fulcrum. To balance a see-saw, for example, two children who weigh the same sit exactly the same distance away from the fulcrum. But a lighter child must create distance—scooting away from the fulcrum—to balance a heavier friend. Archimedes showed King Hieron how he could also use a very long board to create the distance he needed to lift even the heaviest rock with the smallest effort. He playfully boasted, "Give me a place to stand on and I can move the earth!"[6]

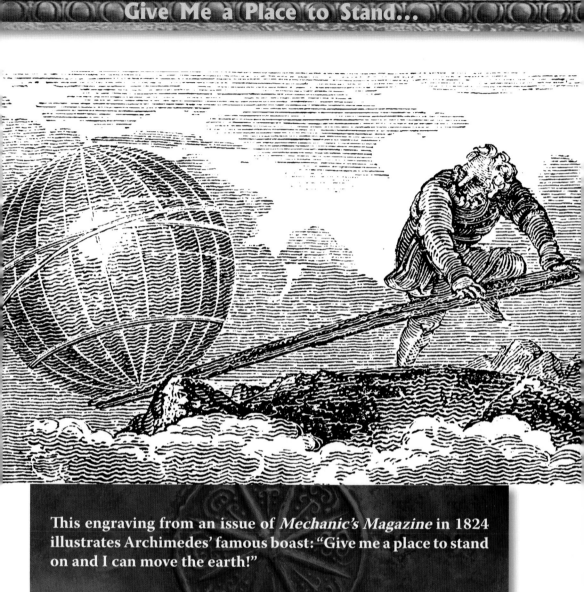

This engraving from an issue of *Mechanic's Magazine* in 1824 illustrates Archimedes' famous boast: "Give me a place to stand on and I can move the earth!"

Archimedes set his discoveries to work on the *Syracusia*, using ropes tied around moving wheels. He may have invented the compound pulley for this very test. On the morning of the challenge, Hieron had a trick up his sleeve. He loaded the ship to the brim with a full cargo of freight and even added passengers, thereby adding tons of additional weight. The confident Archimedes simply reached

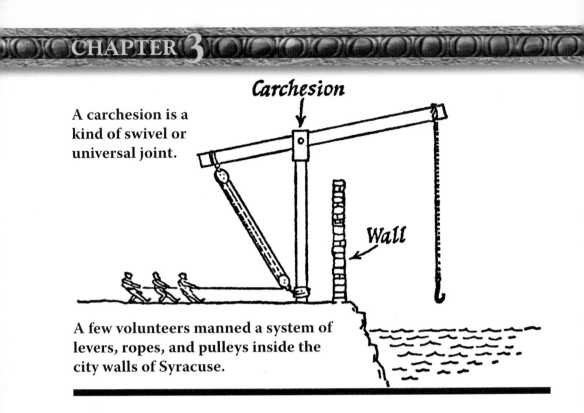

Carchesion

A carchesion is a kind of swivel or universal joint.

Wall

A few volunteers manned a system of levers, ropes, and pulleys inside the city walls of Syracuse.

Archimedes' Claw caught on invading ships as they approached the walls. With a pull, the Syracuse defenders could topple the vessels and make them useless.

down to pick up a single rope. With his gentlest pull, the massive, overburdened ship slid neatly into the harbor with a splash. Awestruck, Hieron declared to the crowd, "From this day forth, we must believe everything that Archimedes says."[7]

The Giants of Science

Ancient Greeks were the first true scientists. They explored the laws of nature, not just to solve problems, but also for the pure joy of thinking, of satisfying their curiosity.

The mathematician **Pythagoras** (6th century BCE) is believed to be the first to call himself a *philosopher*, or "lover of wisdom." Pythagoras and his followers revolutionized the study of triangles, hoping their work would help others explain all of nature using math.

Socrates (470–399 BCE) developed a method of arguing that philosophers, mathematicians, and scientists still use today to find truth.

Aristotle (384–322 BCE) developed a way of thinking, known as logic, that helped thinkers build their arguments piece by piece. Aristotle's logic helped Euclid and Archimedes lay a firm foundation for mathematical proofs.[8]

Aristarchus of Samos (ca. 310–ca. 230 BCE) reasoned that the earth revolves around the sun, long before **Nicolaus Copernicus** proved it in the 16th century.

Democritus (ca. 460–ca. 370 BCE) argued that all things were made of tiny, indivisible particles he called "atoms," long before English teacher John Dalton proposed his atomic theory in 1805.

Greece's first scientist, **Thales of Miletus** (ca. 624–ca. 547 BCE), even wondered if life first came from the ocean, long before Charles Darwin published his theory of evolution in 1859.

The School of Athens fresco by Raphael portrays some of the greatest philosophers of science of ancient times.

Archimedes used his almost limitless skill and creativity to defend his city against the well-armed Roman navy. In this engraving, French historian Andre Thevet (1516–1590) imagines Archimedes plotting his counterattacks with careful measurements on a city map.

CHAPTER 4
The Battle for Syracuse

War raged all around the Mediterranean during the 3rd century BCE. The growing Roman Republic claimed all of present-day Italy and much of the island of Sicily. Meanwhile, the North African nation of **Carthage** looked to expand its power and territory. These two great powers clashed in the three **Punic** Wars between 264 and 146 BCE. In the end, the Mediterranean was only big enough for one of them.

Syracuse sat in the middle of this battle royale. Hieron II struck a deal with Rome. As long as Syracuse promised not to side with Carthage, Rome allowed Syracuse's tradesmen to do business as usual.[1] Archimedes was lucky to live in a city that enjoyed 50 years of peace and prosperity because of this agreement.

But when Hieron died in 215 BCE, his 15-year-old grandson, **Hieronymus**, broke the treaty and declared his support for Carthage. Now Carthage had a stronghold only a boot's kick away from mainland Italy, far too close for Rome's comfort. Rome acted swiftly and severely. They sent their very best general, **Marcus Claudius Marcellus**, to begin the attack on Syracuse in 214 BCE.

The Romans quickly surrounded the city, coming by land through Sicily's territories from the west. Marcellus himself sailed a mighty fleet of warships towards the port. Though Hieronymus had been assassinated by this time, the city remained committed to Carthage. Its leaders turned for help to Archimedes. Now well into his 70s, the aging mathematician reluctantly set his mental play aside. It was time to put math to work to defend his city.

Marcus Claudius Marcellus

Marcellus and his troops sailed into the port of Syracuse in sixty state-of-the-art wooden warships called quinqueremes, powered by 200 rowers.[2] On deck, soldiers suited up for battle. Some heard a faint chuck from the town, and maybe even the whistle a one-ton boulder makes as it flies through the air. A sickening, deafening *crack!* filled the air as the massive rocks punched a gigantic hole through one of the wooden ships.[3] *Chuck! Chuck! Chuck!* came more boulders, flung unseen by Archimedes' new invention—catapults— from behind Syracuse's walls.

Amid the screams of drowning mariners, Marcellus commanded his ships to sail toward the city, out of range of the flying boulders. Smaller catapults pummeled the ships with rocks as they neared shore, breaking sails and oars as well as men. Missiles shot from holes in the city walls reached out over them. So did cranes designed by Archimedes and fitted with ropes and iron claws. Some dropped heavy rocks and boiling liquid onto the enemy ships. Others caught the mighty quinqueremes and overturned them. Suddenly atop the wall a blinding light flashed as Archimedes and his friends arranged curved mirrors to catch the sun's rays. The mirrors turned harmless sunshine into a focused laser, burning the ships.

In a short time Archimedes had turned the Roman navy into a fleet of broken boards. Marcellus's once-fearless troops trembled if they saw anything atop the city's wall, screaming, "Look, Archimedes is aiming one of his machines at us!"[4] Thanks to Archimedes' fearsome inventions, Marcellus could not take Syracuse by sea. The Romans instead settled in for a long blockade. They made a wall with their ships to keep Syracuse from receiving any supplies. The city held out bravely for two years.

In 212 BCE, the proud people decided to celebrate the Feast of Diana in style.[5] As they partied into the night, Roman troops snuck over the walls and opened the town gates. With a trumpet blast, a flood of Roman soldiers poured into Syracuse. They burned the city, took what they liked, and killed whoever got in their way. But Marcellus had given one last order. He commanded his soldiers to bring out Archimedes unharmed.

No one knows for sure what happened next. According to many stories, a soldier found Archimedes at home. Focused on a diagram of circles he had traced on his dirt floor, Archimedes paid no attention to the screaming and destruction going on around him. The soldier commanded Archimedes to leave with him at once. Archimedes looked up, annoyed at how close the soldier was getting to his painstakingly crafted diagram. "Do not disturb my circles!" he

Sun

Mirror

Archimedes'
Heat
Ray

Mirror

Mirror

Archimedes may have used a collection of carefully aimed mirrors as a "death ray" to focus the sun's light into a ship-burning laser. Many scientists—including TV's *Mythbusters*—have tried to recreate this invention, with mixed results.

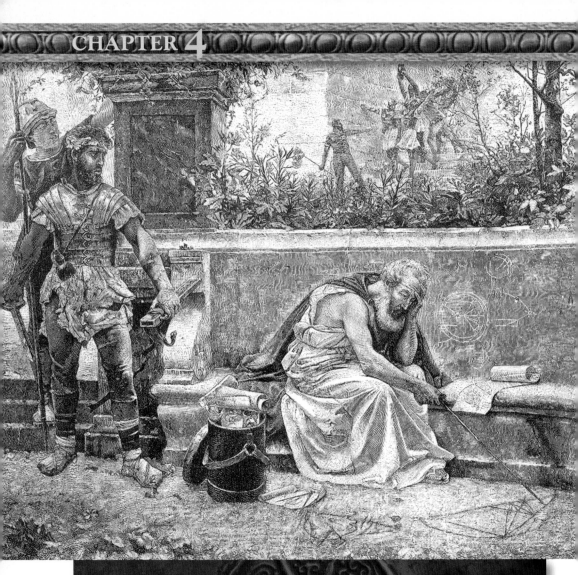

Archimedes traces shapes in the sand, unaware that Marcellus's soldier approaches from behind in this artwork by the French painter Gustave Courtois (1852–1923).

shouted angrily. The hot-tempered soldier had no patience for disobedience. He drew his sword and stabbed Archimedes to death. Legend has it that, as Archimedes lay dying, he uttered, "They've taken away my body, but I shall take away my mind."[6]

Extra, Extra: "News" in Ancient Greece and Rome

Archimedes lived in ancient Greece in the 3rd century BCE, many centuries before the internet or even newspapers. People usually passed news along by word of mouth. Luckily, Archimedes could afford paper, which was rare and expensive. He loved to write letters to his friends to share his findings. More than a dozen of his treatises survive today. Others, unfortunately, have been lost.

What we know of Archimedes, other than his writings about math, comes through Greek and Roman historians like Cicero (106–43 BCE) and **Plutarch** (46–120 CE), who were not even born until after Archimedes had died. Sometimes the truth got muddled by time, and the historians told conflicting stories. Plutarch claims that Archimedes was royalty, related to King Hieron; Cicero says he was just an average person.[7] They do agree that Archimedes died violently during the siege of Syracuse in 212 BCE, the only firm date we know of Archimedes' entire life.

Sources often list Archimedes' birth year as 287 BCE. This year is just a guess, which was made by 12th century poet and scholar John **Tzetzes**. Tzetzes simply chose the age of 75 years, and subtracted it from the established date of Archimedes' death.

Cicero and Discovering the Tomb of Archimedes by British-American painter Benjamin West (1738-1820). In modern times, Archimedes' tomb has never been found.

A Roman soldier stabs the defenseless Archimedes in the back in this art work by P. F. Mola (1612–1666).

CHAPTER 5
Lost and Found

A disappointed Marcellus grieved the loss of this great mind. He sought out Archimedes' friends and relatives, who built the geometric tombstone he had requested. Meanwhile, the stories of Archimedes traveled far and wide and captivated the Roman imagination, celebrating his genius, skill, and strategy.

Roman scholars continued the Greeks' trajectory of learning, but no one could match Archimedes' mental might. When the Roman Empire finally fell in the 5th century CE, its learning and culture fell, too, useless in the hands of Germanic tribes that did not speak or read Greek or Latin. The light of learning in Europe was extinguished for the next thousand years. During these Dark Ages, Europeans cared more about surviving sickness and battle and spreading Christianity than about learning. The papyrus scrolls Archimedes so carefully penned lay gathering dust in libraries until they caught the attention of Arabic mathematicians in the 8th century. After reading *On Floating Bodies*, Arabic shipbuilders created seagoing vessels that were

The Death of Archimedes by French painter Edouard Vimont (1846–1930)

more buoyant than Western ships, possibly giving them an advantage in trade.[1]

While studying in Constantinople in 1453, the German scholar **Regiomontanus** (1436–1476) discovered scrolls containing Archimedes' works. Luckily, Regiomontanus was not only fluent in Greek, but also a mathematician who recognized

Regiomontanus

the importance of what he had found. He translated and published the manuscripts of Archimedes in 1471 for all to see.

Archimedes' ideas sparked the fire of inspiration that transformed the world through Europe's great Scientific Revolution. Nicolaus Copernicus (1473–1543) used Archimedes to prove that the Earth

Nicolaus Copernicus

revolved around the Sun, and not the other way around. German astronomer **Johannes Kepler** (1571–1630) cited Archimedes in his *Laws of Planetary Motion*, the first writings describing the orbits of planets in the solar system. French scientist

Johannes Kepler

Blaise Pascal (1623–1662) used Archimedes' laws on buoyancy to discover hydraulics, used today in everyday things like syringes or brakes in a car. Italian astronomer **Galileo Galilei** (1564–1642) famously said that "without Archimedes, I could have achieved nothing."[2]

Blaise Pascal

Galileo Galilei

Archimedes' work was once again useful, but many scholars feared that some of his manuscripts had been lost forever. In 1906, Danish language scholar **Johan Heiberg** made an exciting find in a Constantinople church. He noticed faint writing between the lines of a medieval prayer book. The writing was Greek, but not Biblical Greek. Heiberg knew this kind of Greek came from ancient Syracuse, and he knew it dealt with math.

The prayers hid seven of Archimedes' treatises, including two that had never been seen by modern eyes. One was *The Stomachion*, which Archimedes wrote as a

Johan Heiberg

37

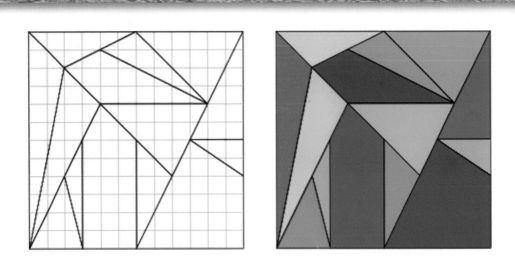

Archimedes' *Stomachion* reads like a 14-piece puzzle, similar to tangrams. Make a copy of this figure and cut out the pieces. How many different ways can you find to make a square?

brainteaser (or, in ancient Greek, a "stomach ache"). How many ways can 14 pieces combine to make a perfect square? Archimedes was dabbling in combinatorics, where the goal is not to find the solution, but to figure out how many different ways a problem can be solved. Combinatorics plays a vital role today in computing and robotics. Before *The Stomachion*, mathematicians thought combinatorics was first invented in the 17th or 18th century.

The other was *The Method of Mechanical Theorems*, in which Archimedes describes a method to find the area under a parabola in a way that resembles modern-day calculus, the mathematical study of changing values. Calculus itself was not discovered until 1687 by Britain's famous mathematician and physicist Sir Isaac Newton, nearly 2,000 years later.[3]

These newly uncovered works confirmed that Archimedes was way ahead of his time. Newton once famously said, "If I have seen further it is by standing on the shoulders of giants." Archimedes was among the very first such "giants." His letters transported his friends into his creative world of shapes, natural truths, and infinite possibilities. They continue to inspire thinkers today.

How the Archimedes Palimpsest Came to Life

In 1229, a monk in Constantinople found a stack of calfskin books, dusty from four centuries of neglect. Sturdy parchment was hard to come by. The monk took the books apart, scraped the pages clean with a knife, and reused them to copy prayers for church services. He had created a palimpsest.

The prayer book sat in the library of the Church of the Holy Sepulchre in Constantinople until a librarian in 1899 noticed Greek peeking from between the prayers. After Johan Heiberg transcribed Archimedes' works seven years later, no one knows what happened to the book, or why it mysteriously showed up at an auction house in New York City in 1988.

By then the prayer book had been badly damaged by mold and by someone who had painted four portraits of saints right onto the pages. Luckily, a wealthy, anonymous collector bought it for $2 million and donated it to the Walters Art Museum in Baltimore. Since then, a team of conservation experts have restored it, and used UV light, X-rays, and computer imaging to reveal more of Archimedes' words. Today the book is on display at the Walters Art Museum, or available to view anytime on Google Books.

Writings of Archimedes

Book of Lemmas

The Cattle-Problem

The Method of Mechanical Theorems

On Circles

On Conoids and Spheroids

On the Equilibrium of Planes

On Floating Bodies

On the Measurement of a Circle

On the Sphere and Cylinder

On Spirals

The Quadrature of the Parabola

The Sand-Reckoner

The Stomachion

TIMELINE

BCE

734   Greeks from Corinth build a new colony at Syracuse on the island of Sicily.

ca. 572–   Greek philosopher Pythagoras revolutionizes the
ca. 497   study of math and geometry.

323–285   Ptolemy I rules Egypt and builds the Mouseoin of Alexandria to house the world's greatest scholars.

ca. 308   Hieron II born in Syracuse.

ca. 300   Greek mathematician Euclid of Alexandria writes *The Elements*.

283–246   Ptolemy II rules as king of Egypt.

ca. 270–215 Hieron II rules as tyrant of Syracuse.

264   The First Punic War between Rome and Carthage begins.

263   Hieron II is forced to sign peace treaty with Rome.

247   Hannibal, a legendary general of Carthage during the Second Punic War, is born; he dies in 183.

241   The First Punic War ends; Rome controls all of Sicily except Syracuse.

218   The Second Punic War begins; Hannibal crosses the Alps and invades Italy.

216	Hieron II dies; his 15-year-old grandson Hieronymos becomes tyrant of Syracuse and declares Syracuse's allegiance to Carthage.
215	Hieronymos is assassinated.
214	Led by General Marcellus, the Roman navy attacks Syracuse, but is defeated by Archimedes' military machines. The Roman navy begins a blockade of Syracuse.
212	Syracuse is captured by Romans; Archimedes is killed.
208	Marcellus dies in battle fighting Hannibal's forces.
201	The Second Punic War ends; Rome gains control of all Carthaginian territory outside of Africa.
149	The Third Punic War begins; Rome destroys Carthage within three years.
75	Cicero discovers and restores Archimedes' tomb.

CE

46	Roman historian Plutarch, who writes *Parallel Lives*, is born; he dies in 120.
1229	A priest, Johannes Myronas, scrapes off parchment containing works of Archimedes and other ancient scholars and uses the paper to copy prayers.
1906	Johan Ludvig Heiberg of Denmark discovers the prayer book; he transcribes it and publishes Archimedes' works.
1988	The Archimedes Palimpsest sells at auction for $2 million to a private collector, who donates it to the Walters Art Museum in Baltimore.
2000–2007	Conservation experts restore the tattered palimpsest, using UV light, X-rays, and computer imaging to uncover the hidden texts.
2008	The Archimedes Palimpsest is published online as a Google Book.

Chapter 1. Eureka!
1. T. L. Heath, *The Works of Archimedes* (Cambridge, United Kingdom: Cambridge University Press, 1897), p. 258.
2. Marcus Tullius Cicero, *The Orations of Marcus Tullius Cicero*, translated by C. D. Yonge (London: George Bell & Sons, 1903), pp. 452–453.

Chapter 2. The Birth of a Thinker
1. Melvyn Bragg, *On Giants' Shoulders*: *Great Scientists and Their Discoveries from Archimedes to DNA* (New York: John Wiley and Sons, 1998), p. 18.
2. Clifford Pickover, *Archimedes to Hawking*: *Laws of Science and the Great Minds Behind Them* (Oxford, United Kingdom: Oxford University Press, 2008), p. 44.
3. Mario Geymonat, *The Great Archimedes*, translated by R. Alden Smith (Waco, Texas: Baylor University Press, 2010), p. 61.
4. Andrew Lawler, Smithsonian.com, "Raising Alexandria," April 2007. http://www.smithsonianmag.com/science-nature/Raising-Alexandria.html

Chapter 3. Give Me a Place to Stand . . .
1. Clifford Pickover, *A Passion for Mathematics*: *Numbers, Puzzles, Madness, Religion, and the Quest for Reality* (Hoboken, New Jersey: John Wiley & Sons, Inc., 2005), p. 292.
2. Dan Q. Posin, *Dr. Posin's Giants*: *Men of Science* (Evanston, Illinois: Row, Peterson, and Company, 1961), p. 9.
3. Pickover, *A Passion for Mathematics*, p. 144.
4. Alan Hirschfeld, *Eureka Man*: *The Life and Legacy of Archimedes* (New York: Walker & Company, 2009), p. 84.
5. Lionel Casson, *Ships and Seamanship in the Ancient World* (Baltimore: The Johns Hopkins University Press, 1995), p. 185.

6. T. L. Heath, *The Works of Archimedes* (Cambridge, United Kingdom: Cambridge University Press, 1897), p. xix.
7. Proclus, *A Commentary on the First Book of Euclid's Elements*, translated by Glenn Raymond Morrow (Princeton, New Jersey: Princeton University Press, 1992), p. 64.
8. Melvyn Bragg, *On Giants' Shoulders: Great Scientists and Their Discoveries from Archimedes to DNA* (New York: John Wiley and Sons, 1998), p. 18.

Chapter 4. The Battle for Syracuse
1. Polybius, The Histories, Volume I, translated by Immanuel Bekker (Boston: Harvard University Press, 1922), pp. 41–43.
2. Stefan G. Chrissanthos, *Warfare in the Ancient World: From the Bronze Age to the Fall of Rome* (Westport, Connecticut: Praeger Publishers, 2008), p. 45.
3. Plutarch, *Plutarch's Lives*, Volume II, translated by John and William Langhorne (New York: Harper & Brothers, 1840), p. 118.
4. Ibid., pp. 121–122.
5. Ibid., p. 123.
6. Paul Hoffman, *Archimedes' Revenge: The Joys and Perils of Mathematics* (New York: Random House, 1997), p. 27.
7. Hazel Muir, editor, *Larousse Dictionary of Scientists* (New York: Larousse, 1994), p. 15.

Chapter 5. Lost and Found
1. Melvyn Bragg, *On Giants' Shoulders: Great Scientists and Their Discoveries from Archimedes to DNA* (New York: John Wiley and Sons, 1998), p. 38.
2. Ibid., p. 23.
3. Anthony Feldman and Peter Ford, *Scientists and Inventors* (London: Bloomsbury Books, 1989), p. 15.

Books

Bancroft-Hunt, Norman. *Living in Ancient Greece*. New York: Chelsea House Publishers, 2009.

Bendick, Jeanne. *Archimedes and the Door of Science*. Bathgate, North Dakota: Bethlehem Books, 2001.

Bordessa, Kris. *Tools of the Ancient Greeks: A Kid's Guide to the History and Science of Life in Ancient Greece*. Norwich, Vermont: Nomad Press, 2006.

Gow, Mary. *Archimedes: Mathematical Genius of the Ancient World*. Berkeley Heights, New Jersey: Enslow Publishers, 2005.

Hasan, Heather. *Archimedes: The Father of Mathematics*. New York: Rosen Publishing Group, 2006.

Hightower, Paul. *The Greatest Mathematician: Archimedes and his Eureka! Moment*. Berkeley Heights, New Jersey: Enslow Publishers, 2009.

Works Consulted

Adam, John A. *Mathematics in Nature: Modeling Patterns in the Natural World*. Princeton, New Jersey: Princeton University Press, 2003.

Bragg, Melvyn. *On Giants' Shoulders: Great Scientists and Their Discoveries from Archimedes to DNA*. New York: John Wiley and Sons, 1998.

Bergmann, Uwe. "Archimedes brought to light." *Physics World*, November 2007, pp. 39-42.
http://www.archimedespalimpsest.org/pdf/physicsworld-november2007.pdf

Casson, Lionel. *Ships and Seamanship in the Ancient World*. Baltimore: The Johns Hopkins University Press, 1995.

Chrissanthos, Stefan G. *Warfare in the Ancient World: From the Bronze Age to the Fall of Rome*. Westport, Connecticut: Praeger Publishers, 2008.

Cicero, Marcus Tullius. *The Orations of Marcus Tullius Cicero*. Translated by C. D. Yonge. London: George Bell & Sons, 1903.

Feldman, Anthony and Peter Ford. *Scientists and Inventors*. London: Bloomsbury Books, 1989.

Geymonat, Mario. *The Great Archimedes*. Translated by R. Alden Smith. Waco, Texas: Baylor University Press, 2010.

Heath, T. L. *The Works of Archimedes*. Cambridge, United Kingdom: Cambridge University Press, 1897.

Hirschfeld, Alan. *Eureka Man: The Life and Legacy of Archimedes*. New York: Walker & Company, 2009.

Hoffman, Paul. *Archimedes' Revenge: The Joys and Perils of Mathematics*. New York: Random House, 1997.

Langone, John, Bruce Stutz, and Andrea Gianpoulos. *Theories for Everything: An Illustrated History of Science from the Invention of Numbers to String Theory*. Washington, D.C.: National Geographic, 2006.

Lawler, Andrew. "Raising Alexandria." *Smithsonian.com*, April 2007. http://www.smithsonianmag.com/science-nature/Raising-Alexandria.html?c=y&page=1

Muir, Hazel (editor). *Larousse Dictionary of Scientists*. New York: Larousse, 1994.

Pickover, Clifford. *Archimedes to Hawking: Laws of Science and the Great Minds Behind Them*. Oxford, United Kingdom: Oxford University Press, 2008.

Pickover, Clifford. *A Passion for Mathematics: Numbers, Puzzles, Madness, Religion, and the Quest for Reality*. Hoboken, New Jersey: John Wiley & Sons, Inc., 2005.

Plutarch. *Plutarch's Lives*, Volume II. Translated by John and William Langhorne. New York: Harper & Brothers, 1840.

Posin, Dan Q. *Dr. Posin's Giants: Men of Science*. Evanston, Illinois: Row, Peterson, and Company, 1961.

Polybius. *The Histories*, Volume I. Translated by Immanuel Bekker. Boston: Harvard University Press, 1922.

Proclus. *A Commentary on the First Book of Euclid's Elements*. Translated by Glenn Raymond Morrow. Princeton, New Jersey: Princeton University Press, 1992.

Vitruvius. *The Ten Books on Architecture*. Translated by Morris Hicky Morgan. London: Oxford University Press, 1914. http://www.gutenberg.org/files/20239/20239-h/29239-h.htm

On the Internet

Archimedes in the 21st Century
https://www.cs.drexel.edu/~crorres/Archimedes/contents.html

The Archimedes Palimpsest
http://archimedespalimpsest.org/

The Story of Mathematics
http://www.storyofmathematics.com/

HowStuffWorks: What was Archimedes' death ray?
http://history.howstuffworks.com/historical-figures/archimedes-death-ray1.htm

Mythbusters: Death Ray MiniMyth
http://dsc.discovery.com/tv-shows/mythbusters/videos/death-ray-minimyth.htm

NOVA: Infinite Secrets
http://www.pbs.org/wgbh/nova/archimedes/

PHONETIC PRONUNCIATIONS

Archias (AR-kee-us)
Archimedes (AR-kim-EE-deez)
Aristarchus (AIR-iss-TARK-us)
Aristotle (AIR-iss-TOT-ull)
Blaise Pascal (BLAZE PASS-cal)
Carthage (KAR-thaj)
Cicero (SIS-er-oh)
Corinth (KOR-inth)
Cyrene (SY-reen)
Democritus (dim-OK-rit-us)
Eratosthenes
    (air-uh-TOSS-then-eez)
Euclid (YOOK-lid)
Eureka (yoo-REE-kah)
Galileo Galilei (gal-ill-LAY-oh
    gal-ill-LAY)
Hieron (HY-ur-on)
Hieronymus (hy-RON-im-us)
Johan Heiberg (YO-hahn
    HY-burg)
Johannes Kepler (yo-HAH-ness
    KEP-lur)

Marcus Claudius Marcellus
    (MARK-us CLOD-ee-us
    mar-SELL-us)
Miletus (my-LEET-us)
Nicolaus Copernicus (NIK-oh-
    laos koh-PUR-nik-us)
Ortygia (or-TIJ-ee-uh)
Phidias (FID-ee-us)
Plutarch (PLOO-tark)
Ptolemy (TALL-em-ee)
Punic (PYOO-nik)
Pythagoras (pie-THAG-or-us)
Regiomontanus
    (REJ-ee-oh-MONT-an-us)
Samos (SAM-ohss)
Sicily (SIS-ill-ee)
Socrates (SOCK-rah-teez)
Syracuse (SEE-ra-KYOOZ)
Thales (THAY-leez)
Tzetzes (TSEE-tsis)

apprentice (ah-PREN-tiss)—A person who learns a trade by working for someone already in that trade.

blockade (blaw-KAYD)—A military operation in which an area is isolated so that neither entry nor exit is possible; used to starve the target into submission.

buoyancy (BOY-uhn-see)—Floating in a fluid.

circumference (sir-KUM-fur-ens)—The distance around a circle.

diameter (dy-AM-uh-tuhr)—The distance across a circle.

displace (dis-PLACE)—To be pushed out of place by something else.

equations (ee-KWAY-zhuns)—Demonstrations that two things are equal, with a = sign joining them.

fulcrum (FULL-krum)—The pivot point around which a lever moves.

googol (GOO-gull)—A very large number, written as a 1 followed by one hundred zeroes.

palimpsest (PAL-imp-sest)—A parchment used more than once; previous text has been erased and overwritten, but sometimes is still visible.

perimeter (pehr-IH-muh-tehr)—The length of a continuous line around a geometric figure.

planetarium (plan-uh-TAIR-ee-um)—A model that represents a planetary system.

postulate (POS-tyoo-leht)—A rule that is obviously true on its own and does not need to be proven.

quinquereme (KWIN-kwuh-reem)—Roman warship with two or three banks of oars and five oarsmen on each bank.

siege (SEEJ)—A military operation that surrounds a target to cut it off from outside help; can last for weeks or even months.

treatise (TREE-tiss)—A formal, detailed essay on a scholarly topic.